Tibetan Manuscripts

T0366891

Sam Fogg Rare Books and Manuscripts
15d Clifford Street
London W1S 4JZ

TEL	020 7534 2100
FAX	020 7534 2122
E-MAIL	info@samfogg.com
WEBSITE	www.samfogg.com

Tibet, hidden in the centre of Asia by some of the highest mountains in the world, has one of the most inhospitable environments on earth. Compared to the size of its population, the amount of literary works preserved in Tibetan is truly amazing. What is perhaps even more remarkable is the nature of this huge literary corpus. Most of the preserved Tibetan literature originates in the concern of its author or translators with religious matters, particularly Buddhist and Bon, the two most important religious traditions practiced in Tibet.

The introduction, in the second half of the seventh century, of an alphabet derived most probably from a north-Indian script, is traditionally attributed to Tönmi Sambhota (Thon-mi Sambhota). The alphabet allowed for Tibetan to be written down and for the first written translations of Buddhist texts to be produced. Tönmi Sambhota was a minister of the emperor Songtsen gampo (Srong-brtsan sgam-po), who allegedly introduced Buddhism to Tibet. Modern historians have observed that the use of a form of writing was a necessary prerequisite for the administrative organization of an empire that in the following century was able to defeat the Chinese and sack their capital Xi'an. Whatever preoccupation came first, the translation of Buddhist literature from Sanskrit and Chinese or the use of the written language for the administration of the Tibetan empire, the close link between Buddhism and the origins of writing in Tibet is undeniable. The

Tibetan manuscripts found in Dunhuang, which are one of the most relevant groups of writings dating back to the period of the Tibetan empire in the ninth century, reflect this double function of the written language, being partly of a religious nature and partly of a historical and administrative nature.

During the reign of Tri Songdetsen (Khri Srong-lde-brtsan) in the second half of the eight century, the translation of Buddhist texts became a state-sponsored and strictly regulated activity, with its centre in Samye (bSam-yas), the first monastery established in Tibet. Here tradition places the famous council of Samye. According to later Tibetan historiography, the emperor Tri Songdetsen, having staged a debate between Indian and Chinese monks, eventually banned the Chinese party and their teachings. In 842 CE the assassination of the emperor Langdarma (Glang-dar-ma) by a Buddhist monk after a persecution of Buddhism marked the end of the Tibetan empire, the first centralized government of Tibet, and plunged the country into a dark period of political instability and religious decline, during which probably not much was written.

The beginning of the second diffusion of Buddhism in Tibet in the eleventh century saw a revival of translations and literary activities. It was connected with the new texts imported by Tibetan Buddhist scholars and practitioners, who went to India to study, and by Indian masters who came to Tibet to teach. In the absence of a strong centralized government, Indian Buddhism became the most important shaping factor for all subsequent phases of Tibetan culture. Once the ordination of monks was re-established in Tibet, some of the old monasteries were restored and new ones were founded, each one transmitting the specific teachings collected or received from India by their founders. Monasteries become the economical, political, cultural and religious centres around which life was organized. Most of the doctrines transmitted by the various schools of Tibetan Buddhism are esoteric and therefore require oral instructions and consecrations before the actual texts can be memorised, understood and practiced. Secret teachings were difficult to get and students were expected to pay their teachers for them. The famous translator and spiritual master Marpa (Mar-pa, 1012–1096) decided to go to India to collect teachings and books because his Tibetan teacher Drokmi ('Brog-mi, 992–1072) was too expensive (See Roerich, *The Blue Annals*, p. 208). Huge collections of books were assembled in the monastic libraries. The control of the library of a famous master could lead to bitter disputes among his pupils. An example of this is the quarrel over the possession of the library once belonging to the master Pakmodrupa (Phag-mo-gru-pa, 1110–1170), recorded by Gö lotsawa ('Gos lo-tsa-ba, 1392–1481) in *The Blue Annals* (See Roerich, *The Blue Annals*, p. 620). Books, as long as their teachings were correctly transmitted, formed one of the symbolic capitals of the monasteries, and legitimised the religious and temporal authority of their abbots.

Some schools of Tibetan Buddhism, in particular the Nyingmapa (rNying-ma-pa), who continued to follow the Buddhist teachings that had reached Tibet during the first diffusion of Buddhism, have a very special connection with books. According to their beliefs, some books were hidden during the persecution of Buddhism at the time of the emperor Langdarma, in order to be rediscovered later, in more peaceful times. These texts, called *terma* (*gter-ma*), once rediscovered had the status of legitimate Buddhist teachings. In many cases the texts were discovered in the form of actual manuscripts by particularly powerful masters, who had received revelations about the places to look for them. In some other cases, however, the text could be directly revealed in a dream to the master.

We have seen that the transmission of teachings and the legitimisation of the spiritual authority of the monks was one of the functions books were supposed to carry in Tibetan Buddhism. These were not, however, the main concerns of the monastic communities. Only a relatively small fraction of the monks had a scholastic training and books had important roles in the daily routine of recitations practiced in the monasteries. Moreover books could became objects of veneration and of offerings, playing the same role as statues, paintings or *stupas*. In fact,

following the classical Buddhist distinction between body, speech and mind, images represented the body of the Buddha, *stupas* represented his mind and books his speech.

For lay Tibetan communities manuscripts could provide help in the daily recitations of prayers and could be objects of veneration in domestic shrines. They had also a further important function. As in the case of statues and paintings, donors of one or more volumes to a monastery could gain great merits for themselves, their families and all sentient beings. Commissions were placed to professional scribes, who would copy the selected texts and prepare the new volumes for the donations. Inevitably also a certain amount of social prestige was attached to such donations and donors' names were sometimes recorded in the colophons of the volumes.

In light of what we have said of the varied and multifaceted functions of books in pre-modern Tibetan society, it becomes quite easy to understand why volumes were produced with such perfect workmanship, using only the best materials and so lavishly decorated. In some cases, as for instance in a *Prajnaparamita* manuscript still preserved in the monastery of Gyantse (Fig. 1), the sheer size of the manuscripts could reach quite amazing proportions, with pages more than one metre wide. Of the two main forms of the Tibetan alphabet, the *ucen* (*dbu-can*) regular style and the *ume* (*dbu-med*) cursive,

Fig. 1. The famous Prajnaparamita
sutra manuscript preserved in Gyantse
monastery, Dorje Ying Lhakhang.

of this tradition. Gold and silver manuscripts on blue paper were produced also in Nepal and it is not clear if they represent an Indian tradition or an influence from contemporary Tibetan manuscripts.

Manuscripts were sometimes illustrated, normally in the first and last page and only very rarely throughout the text. Illustrated pages were often protected by a silk cloth stitched to the upper edge of the page. The first page, normally written in larger and more decorated letters than the rest of the text, bears the title of the volume. In the case of translations, normally from Sanskrit or from Chinese, the title is generally inscribed first in the original language, transcribed using Tibetan letters, and then translated into Tibetan. Following the Indian tradition of book illumination, the subjects of the illustrations are normally iconic depictions of deities represented in square vignettes at the left and right edges of the page or in the middle of it. Narrative paintings, a genre rarely encountered in Tibetan painting in general, are extremely rare in book illustration. One explanation for this could be that most of the texts illustrated have either a philosophical or ritual character and generally do not lend themselves to narrative painting. The choice of preferring iconic illustrations to narrative paintings also reflects the significance of the books as relics of the presence of the Buddha in his speeches. Assemblies of bodhisattvas, deities and monks surrounding a preaching Buddha, which represent the setting for the speech of the

only the former was used to copy canonical religious texts because its more time-consuming execution provided greater merits for the donor. Only two of the manuscripts in the exhibition, nos 1 and 4, are written in *ume*. They are both copies of non-canonical texts. In some of the best manuscripts the pages were stained dark blue or black and carefully polished before being inscribed using gold and silver inks. This practice, attested in Tibet since the very beginning of the second diffusion of Buddhism, could have had a far-eastern origin, with its prototypes in the Chinese copies of the *sutras* on blue paper. Manuscript no. 21 is an outstanding example

Buddha recorded in the text, although common in Chinese copies of the *sutras* (as can be seen in the first volume of manuscript no. 21), are not normally present in Tibetan manuscripts. Two kinds of subjects, the lineages of the masters who transmitted the teachings contained in the text and the portraits of the donors of the volume, seem, on the other hand, to be a peculiarity of the Tibetan tradition of Buddhist book illumination. Lineages of masters are illustrated in manuscript no. 13, where a Taklungpa lineage appears, and in manuscript no. 16, that has a Karmapa lineage. Donors' portraits can be seen on one page of manuscript no. 9. These two kinds of illustrations reflect on one hand the acute concern of the schools of Tibetan Buddhism about the legitimacy of their teachings and on the other hand the relevance of the social prestige connected with the donation of books. Given the rather traditionalist approach to the art of writing in Tibetan culture, the pictorial style of the illustration is often the only clue to the date of production of the volume in which they appear.

Even the structure of Tibetan books shows the acknowledgement of the indebtedness to Indian traditions. Although the materials used were very different, the Indian format of the *pothi* was adopted for most Tibetan manuscripts. In an Indian *pothi* manuscript a number of palm-leaf unbound pages are kept together by one or two strings piercing through

Fig. 2. A section of the library in Gyantse monastery, Dorje Ying Lhakhang.

the manuscript and through the two usually wooden covers at the top and bottom of the volume. Manuscripts nos 19 and 20 are two examples of this type of book, one from India and the other from Nepal. The *pothi* format originated in India but was diffused also in other countries, such as Nepal, whose culture was influenced by India. Tibetan manuscripts are normally written on locally produced paper, with the pages wider than long in order to imitate the shape, if not the size and the proportions, of Indian palm-leaf pages. They are protected by two wooden covers at the top and the bottom of the stack but they are not pierced by any string. In many manuscripts it is still possible to see on each page one or two circles to mark the places where an Indian manuscript would have been pierced, as can be seen in manuscripts no. 5, 8 and 16 of this exhibition.

Woodblock printing, a technique introduced in Tibet from China, was used in the production of books and for the under-drawings of some sets of paintings (*thang-ka*). Some monasteries kept huge sets of blocks, mostly of Buddhist canonical literature, but also of other texts, like the guide to the monastery. As Tucci narrates, visitors to these monasteries had to provide the paper and, for a small fee, could ask to have the volumes they were interested in printed for them. Item no. 18 is an outstanding example of an illustrated block printed book produced in the Narthang monastery (sNar-thang)

Book covers, that in principle could be just two wooden boards, were sometimes highly decorated, as can be seen in item no. 22 of this exhibition. They could be painted and carved both on the outer and on the inner face. In some rare cases they were covered with metal sheets, normally gilded copper but sometimes silver, worked in *repoussé*. More normally the outer faces of the wooden covers were gilded. Due to the particular way in which volumes

were stacked in monastic libraries, piled on racks with only one of the short sides showing, book covers were often decorated on one of the short sides (Fig. 2). A particularly deep carving on the short side of a set of book covers can be observed in manuscript no. 8. Here is also normally carved the letter of the Tibetan alphabet used to number the volumes in a large collection, like a section of the Buddhist canon. Manuscripts could otherwise be labelled by stitching a small piece of cloth to one of the short side edges of the first page. On this cloth, which would be hanging in front of the short side of the volume, the numbering of the volume or an abbreviation of its title would have been recorded. Therefore they would have been accessible when the volume was stacked on the rack in the library. Manuscripts nos 8 and 16 still preserve these kind of labels.

Manuscripts, as we have seen, constitute an absolutely central aspect of Tibetan culture and one of its most sophisticated achievements. They not only transmit some of the deepest philosophical and religious ideas ever thought, but also shed light on the political, social and artistic concerns of the people who produced them. Tibetan manuscripts are a precious testimony of a civilization that in this century has been in great danger and has almost disappeared from its homeland.

Aldo Mignucci
London, October 2001.

1 Hymns praising the Great Symbol
(*Mahamudra*)

Paper
80 × 205 mm
First page illustrated and diagrams
in the text
Text in Tibetan
Central Tibet
12th–13th century

The body of the text of this small
manuscript, written in cursive script
(*ume, dbu-med*), consists of hymns
praising the Great Symbol
(*mahamudra*) system of meditation.
The manuscript contains a 'spell
wheel' (*mantracakra*) for the
destruction of demons and averting
evil. The first page is an example of
drawing at the beginning of the second
diffusion of Buddhism in Tibet.
It represents on the left side the
bodhisattva Vajradhara and the
Buddha Sakyamuni on the right, with

an altar surmounted by three *stupas*
and surrounded by offerings in the
middle. Stylistically the drawing
belongs to the group of Tibetan
objects influenced by the North-
Eastern Indian Pala style, as can be
seen in the details of the ornaments
and of the crown worn by Vajradhara.
The altar with the offerings is
remarkably similar to those normally
represented in the consecration scenes
in one of the two lower corners of
Tibetan *thang-kas* of the twelfth and
thirteenth centuries.

2 The White Lotus of Compassion Sutra
(SKT *Arya karunapundarika nama
mahayana sutra*, TIB *'Phags pa snying
rje padma dkar po shes bya ba theg pa
chen po'i mdo*)

Wood and paper
265 ff
241 × 686 mm
2 illuminations
Text in Tibetan
Central Tibet
12th–13th century

This volume of the *Karunapundarika
Sutra* is a remarkable example of book-
production at the beginning of the
second diffusion of Buddhism in
Tibet. The text of this canonical
Mahayana *sutra* (sDe-dge (Ui *et al.*)
112, Beijing (Suzuki) 780, Ulan Bator
(Bethlenfalvy) 92) is copied in gold on
blue paper in an exquisitely balanced
and neat hand. The first page is

illustrated with an image of Sakyamuni
on the left and the *bodhisattva*
Vairocana (rNam-par snang-byed) on
the right. These two paintings display
all the characteristics of the Central-
Tibetan style based on the
contemporary Pala style of North-
eastern India. The manuscript can
therefore be dated to the twelfth or the
beginning of the thirteenth century.

3 First page of a Perfection of Wisdom in
One Hundred Thousand Verses
(TIB *'Phags pa shes rab kyi pha rol tu
phyin pa stong phrag brgya pa*)

Paper
220 × 665 mm
Illuminated
Text in Tibetan
Tibet
13th century

This imposing title page for a
manuscript of the largest version in
one hundred thousand verses of the
Prajnaparamita Sutra has three
lines of alternating gold and silver
calligraphy on black paper. The two
miniatures at the left and the right
of the text represent pairs of deities
above a Sanskrit silver inscription in
Lantsa script containing *mantras*, all
in a distinctive Pala-influenced style,
that points to a date in the thirteenth
century.

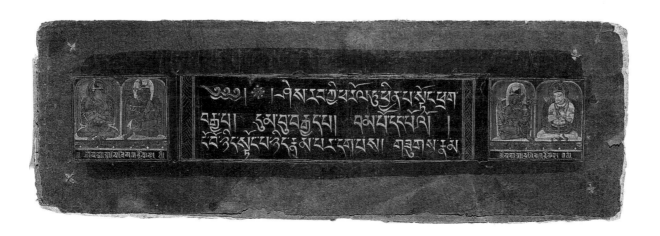

4   Commentary on the Light from the
Lamp of Awareness
(TIB *gZhi lam 'bras bu'i rnam bzhags la
chos kyi gter mdzod chen po kun 'dus rig
pa'i sgron ma'i 'od*)

Wood and paper
201 + 2 ff
100 × 332 mm
4 miniatures
Text in Tibetan
Tibet
13th century

This non-canonical instruction text
concerns the philosophy of the Great
Perfection, a system followed in Tibet
both by some Buddhist schools and by
the Bon-pos. It is copied in a beautiful
cursive calligraphy (*ume, dbu-med*)
in black and red on cream paper.
The illuminations on the first page
represent the primordial Buddha
Samantabhadra and Vajrasattva, in a
heavily shaded and brilliantly coloured
style that show its indebtedness to
East-Indian Pala paintings and
points to a date of production in the
thirteenth century. The two miniatures
in the last page represent two lamas
who transmitted the teachings and,
although not inscribed, could be the
two authors of the text, mentioned as
Shag-kya'i dge'-sbyong and the monk
Shag-kya rdo-rje in the colophon. The
radiocarbon (C^{14}) dating of the covers
of this manuscript to 965–1163 CE.
seems a bit too early if compared to the
style of its illustrations. This however
could be explained considering the
preciousness of wood in Central
Tibet: since it had to be imported
from Eastern Tibet or from the South,
it is possible that some earlier wood
was used at a later stage to produce
these covers.

5   Recitation of the Names of the Noble
Manjusri
(SKT *Arya manjusri nama sangiti*,
TIB *'Phags pa 'jam dpal gyi mtshan
brjod*)

Paper
26 ff
126 × 348 mm
4 miniatures
Text in Tibetan
Tibet
13th century

Although this manuscript has now lost
its covers, it is an excellent example of
Tibetan book-production of the early
thirteenth century in gold calligraphy
on blue paper. The tantric text of
invocations to the *bodhisattva*
Manjusri is decorated with four vibrant
miniatures, representing a form of
Manjusri and Avalokitesvara on the
first page and Vajrapani and Acala on
the last one, executed in an early
version of the Nepalese style current
in Central and Southern Tibet at the
beginning of the thirteenth century.
These paintings are so close to the
style of contemporary Nepalese
manuscript illuminations that it is
possible to hypothesize that they were
produced by a Newari artist, working
probably in Tibet for a Tibetan patron.

6   Recitation of the Names of the Noble
Manjusri
(SKT *Arya manjusri nama sangiti*,
TIB *'Phags pa 'jam dpal gyi mtshan
brjod*)

Wood and paper
44 ff, some missing
70 × 160 mm
Illuminated book cover
Text in Tibetan
Tibet
13th century

This delightful small manuscript
was most probably produced for
the personal use of its first owner,
as shown by the well worn and
patinated covers and the present lack
of the original numbered pagination,
due to the constant rubbing of fingers
turning the pages. The exquisite
painted decoration on the inner
face of the top cover represents the
'Seven emblems of royalty' stemming
from a bejewelled vase, a classical
Indian theme. The substitution of
the wise minister, one of the seven
emblems, with an image of Kubera,
the god of wealth, is sometimes
encountered in Tibetan paintings at
the beginning of the second diffusion
of Buddhism. The style of this
painting, with a strong Nepalese
influence in the lotuses on which
the figures sit, in the details of the
cushions behind the figures and
in the treatment of the background
space filled with flowers, points to
a thirteenth century date.

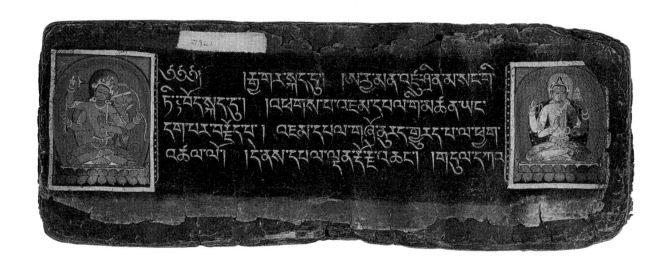

7 The Perfection of Wisdom in Eight Thousand Verses
(SKT *Arya astasahasrikaprajnapara-mita*, TIB *'Phags pa shes rab kyi pha rol tu phyin pa brgyad stong pa*)

Paper
314 ff
200 × 650 mm
Text in Tibetan
Tibet
13th–14th century

Although this manuscript is not illustrated, it displays some of the best *ucen* calligraphy produced in Tibet. The gold letters are pleasingly spaced and very exactly executed on the lustrous blue ground, which represent 'the clear empty space, the void from which all things arise'. The manuscript shows some archaic orthographic characteristics, such as the presence of the *da-drag* (the letter 'da' as a secondary suffix for some syllables), which point to an early date, probably in the thirteenth or fourteenth century. The text is a canonical Buddhist *sutra*, central to Mahayana teachings (sDe-dge (Ui *et al.*) 12, Beijing (Suzuki) 734, Ulan Bator (Bethlenfalvy) 12).

8 The Perfection of Wisdom in Eight Thousand Verses
(SKT *Arya astasahasrikaprajnapara-mita*, TIB *'Phags pa shes rab kyi pha rol tu phyin pa brgyad stong pa*)

Wood and paper
353 ff
222 × 695 mm
34 miniatures
Text in Tibetan
Nepal, Dolpo
14th century

This and the following manuscripts (nos 8–12) are outstanding examples of books produced in Dolpo, one of the two main Tibetan enclaves in Nepal, between the fourteenth and fifteenth centuries. They share some common features, like the deeply carved decorations on the short sides of the book covers and the style of the painted decorations, which moves from an earlier Nepalese style comparable to the fourteenth century paintings produced in Nepal, to a style that, retaining its basic Nepalese features, adds some elements derived from Chinese Buddhist painting. The style of these paintings shares many common features with that of the murals still preserved in Mustang, the other Nepalese region of Tibetan culture, in the Lori Stupa and in the Lo Jampa Lhakang. Most of the surviving Dolpo manuscripts are not illustrated and, when they are, generally have two miniatures at the beginning of the volume and two on the last page. This copy of the *Prajnaparamita Sutra* (sDe-dge (Ui *et al.*) 12, Beijing (Suzuki) 734, Ulan Bator (Bethlenfalvy) 12) opens with a title page in gold on blue paper, protected by a paper flap. The two illustrations, of Sakyamuni on the left and his two assistants on the right, except for their much larger size, are directly comparable to the Buddha images on one of the covers of the fourteenth century Nepalese *Pancaraksa* manuscript in this exhibition (no. 19). The rest of the manuscript is then copied on white Tibetan paper in black, with red circles to mark the place where a Nepalese manuscript in palm leaves would have been pierced, and it is profusely illustrated. Some images have been cut out of the page, probably to be used as amulets. The scribbles, small graffiti and calligraphy exercises found on some of the pages of the manuscript suggest that it has been used for teaching, probably to very young novices.

9 Five hymns addressed to five protective Buddhist goddesses
(SKT *Pancaraksa*) and *Mahasannipataratnaketudharani*

Wood and paper
294 ff
210 × 650 mm
25 miniatures
Text in Tibetan
Nepal, Dolpo
14th century

This Dolpo manuscript, which combines the text of the *Mahasannipataratnaketudharani*, a Mahayana sutra, with that of the *Pancaraksa*, the hymns to five protective Buddhist goddesses, is profusely decorated at the beginning and the end of each section with illuminated pages bearing one painting on the left and one on the right. *Pancaraksa* manuscripts, being formed by a collection of five texts, to which a sixth text is added in this volume, seem to be more profusely illuminated than most of the other illustrated Dolpo manuscripts since the rule of two miniatures on the first page and two on the last one applies to each section of the book. The title pages of each section are copied in gold on dark blue paper and are protected by a paper flap over the writing. The rest of the pages are in black on beige Tibetan paper. The style of the paintings mixes typically Newari motifs and palette with some Chinese influences, that can be seen for instance in the richer and more volumetric treatment of the garments of the Buddhas. This style points to a fourteenth century date for the manuscript, perhaps somewhat later than the previous item. The presence of a consecration scene on one section's closing pages, in which the donors of the manuscript are portrayed and identified by inscriptions, is a typically Tibetan subject in Buddhist book illumination and reflects the social prestige connected with the donation of books in Tibetan society.

10   The Perfection of Wisdom in Eight
Thousand Verses
(SKT *Arya astasahasrikaprajnapara-
mita*, TIB *'Phags pa shes rab kyi pha rol
tu phyin pa brgyad stong pa*)

Wood and paper
343 ff
220 × 650 mm
4 miniatures
Text in Tibetan
Nepal, Dolpo
14th–15th century

This copy of the *Eight Thousand
Verses Prajnaparamita Sutra* (sDe-
dge (Ui *et al.*) 12, Beijing (Suzuki) 734,
Ulan Bator (Bethlenfalvy) 12) is
illustrated in the first and last page, a
typical feature of illuminated Dolpo
manuscripts. The title page, the only
one in gold on blue paper, has two
miniatures representing Sakyamuni
and Amitayus, seated on lion thrones
and accompanied by their respective
attendants. The figures are

surrounded by red halos, decorated
with a darker red scrollwork, a typical
Nepalese feature. Their garments,
however, like those of the Sadaksari
and green Tara figures that appear
on the last page, are depicted with
a greater emphasis on the folds and
with more naturalistically represented
scarves. These stylistic features
suggest a date towards the end of the
fourteenth or the beginning of the
fifteenth century.

11   Five hymns addressed to five
protective Buddhist goddesses
(SKT *Pancaraksa*) and
Mahasannipataratnaketudharani

Wood and paper
323 ff
220 × 660 mm
24 miniatures
Text in Tibetan
Nepal, Dolpo
14th–15th century

Each title page and final page of the six
sections of this text, comprising the
Mahasannipataratnaketudharani and
the *Pancaraksa* cycle, is illustrated
with a painting on the left and one
on the right. The title pages of each
section are written in gold on dark blue
or black paper and the writing is
protected by paper flaps. Their
illuminations represent Buddhas and
the five goddesses to whom the
Pancaraksa hymns are dedicated,
while the last pages are reserved for

bodhisattvas and protective deities.
The first page of the first section, the
Mahasannipataratnaketudharani,
has on the left a crowned image of
Sakyamuni, identified by a caption,
and a teaching Buddha on the right.
They are accompanied by two
attendants each and they are seated
on lotuses against a richly decorated
throne back, all in a typically Nepalese-
influenced style from the end of the
fourteenth or the beginning of the
fifteenth century.

12   The Perfection of Wisdom in Eight
Thousand Verses
(SKT *Arya astasahasrikaprajnapara-
mita*, TIB *'Phags pa shes rab kyi pha rol
tu phyin pa brgyad stong pa*) with
Pancaraksa illustrations

Wood and paper
About 340 ff, incomplete
210 × 610 mm
illustrated
Text in Tibetan
Nepal, Dolpo
15th century

This Dolpo manuscript of the *Eight
Thousand Verses Prajnaparamita
Sutra* (sDe-dge (Ui *et al.*) 12,
Beijing (Suzuki) 734, Ulan Bator
(Bethlenfalvy) 12) is preserved between
two beautifully carved wooden covers.
The Sanskrit inscription on the top
cover is the *Pratityasamutpada gatha*,
one of the most famous verses of
Mahayana literature, often used in the
consecration of ritual objects. The
manuscript itself is not illustrated but

six painted pages, also produced in
Dolpo, have been added to it. One
represents Bhaisajyaguru, the Buddha
of medicine on the left and the
bodhisattva Vajrapani on the right,
while the others are title pages from
a *Pancaraksa* manuscript, with
illustration of the Buddhas of the
five Families and the five protective
goddesses. These lively paintings are
fine examples of fifteenth century
illuminations from Dolpo.

13 The Paradise of Noble Amitabha
(SKT *Amitabhavyuha mahayana sutra*,
TIB *'Phags pa 'od dpag med kyi bkod pa
zhes bya ba theg pa chen po'i mdo*)

Wood and paper
83 ff
110 × 330 mm
23 miniatures
Text in Tibetan
Central Tibet
early 15th century

This unusual manuscript in gold on brown Chinese Daphne paper stained black in the area occupied by the writing was produced for the Taklung (sTag-lung) order, one of the sub-schools of the Kagyupa (bKa-brgyud-pa) order of Tibetan Buddhism. The text is a canonical Mahayana *sutra* describing Sukhavati, the western paradise, or Pure Land, of Amitabha, the Buddha of Boundless Light. The twenty three miniatures, in a technique reminiscent of the black *thang-ka* production of Tibetan paintings, are inscribed in cursive script (*dbu-med*) with the names of the figures portrayed. They represent Akshobhya, Ratnasambhava, Amitabha and Amoghasiddhi, four of the Buddhas of the five families, and a lineage of masters of the monastery of Taklung, which, although the names are in some cases different from those found in *The Blue Annals*, seems to extend to the beginning of the fifteenth century, the period in which this copy of the manuscript must have been produced. The top book cover is stylistically more ancient than the manuscript and appears to be a replacement of the original cover, now lost.

14 The Perfection of Wisdom in Eight Thousand Verses
(SKT *Arya astasahasrikaprajnapara-mita*, TIB *'Phags pa shes rab kyi pha rol tu phyin pa brgyad stong pa*)

Wood and paper
347 ff
190 × 680 mm
28 miniatures
Text in Tibetan
Central Tibet
early 15th century

This profusely illustrated copy of the *Prajnaparamita Sutra in Eight Thousand Verses* (sDe-dge (Ui *et al.*) 12, Beijing (Suzuki) 734, Ulan Bator (Bethlenfalvy) 12) opens with a magnificent title page decorated by an image of Prajnaparamita on the left and one of Sakyamuni on the right, both seated on lion thrones and flanked by their attendants. This page is protected by one layer of orange Chinese silk and one of yellow Indian silk. The stylistic features of the images, representing Buddhas and *bodhisattvas*, show a basically Nepalese style in its brilliant colours and flourishing motifs, to which some Chinese elements, such as the more volumetric treatment of the robes, are added. The synthesis of the more ancient Nepalese and Pala styles with new currents from China at the beginning of the fifteenth century paves the way for the emergence of the later schools of Tibetan painting. This manuscript represents one of the early attempts in this direction and can therefore be dated to the early fifteenth century.

15 The King of Contemplation Sutra
(SKT *Arya sarva dharma svabhava samatavipancita samadhi rajanama mahayana sutra*, TIB *'Phags pa chos thams cad kyi rang bzhin mnyam pa nyid rnam par spros pa'i ting nge 'dzin gyi rgyal po zhes bya ba theg pa chen po'i mdo*)

Paper
311 ff
180 × 580 mm
First page illustrated and 14 other miniatures
Text in Tibetan
Tibet
15th century

The presence of an image of Padmasambhava on the title page of this richly decorated manuscript in gold letters on black paper proves that it was produced for a Nyingmapa (rNying-ma-pa) monastery, the order of Tibetan Buddhism that follows the teachings introduced during the first diffusion of Buddhism in Tibet between the seventh and the ninth centuries. The unusual style of the paintings, in which Nepalese motifs, like the structure of the throne of the Buddha on the first page, are mixed with a few Chinese elements, like the way the inner robe of the same Buddha is tied and the more volumetric representation of garments, points to a date in the beginning of the fifteenth century and perhaps to a centre of production in Eastern Tibet. This interesting style seems to be one of the first attempts to reintroduce some Chinese pictorial elements in Tibetan painting and this manuscript may prove to be one of the seminal works in the development of the later Tibetan schools of painting. The text is a canonical Mahayana sutra (sDe-dge (Ui *et al.*) 127, Beijing (Suzuki) 795, Ulan Bator (Bethlenfalvy) 117).

16   The Sutra of the Auspicious Aeon
(SKT *Bhadrakalpika sutra*, TIB *'Phags pa bskal pa bzang po pa*)

Wood and paper
297 ff
215 × 660 mm
Most of the pages illuminated
Text in Tibetan
Central Tibet
15th–16th century

This sumptuously illustrated manuscript in silver and gold on black paper was produced for the Karmapa sub-school of the Kagyupa order. The lineage of the Karmapas, up to Chodrak Gyatso (1450–1506), the seventh Karmapa, appears on f. 212 of the manuscript and the volume was probably produced during his lifetime, perhaps at Tsurpu, the main seat of the Karmapas. The volume opens with a magnificent first page, in which the Tibetan title of the text, protected by a peacock feather canopy and sitting on a lotus, is flanked by an image of Sakyamuni on the left and one of Amitayus on the right, each in his own shrine and with his own attendants. The distinctive angular style of the calligraphy is illuminated by scrollwork in raised gold pigment in the thick lines forming the letters. Most of the following pages are illustrated on the verso with small Buddha images, stupas, mahasiddhas or dharmapalas. Page 295 is illustrated with a scene of consecration. This is one of the most lavishly illustrated among surviving Tibetan manuscripts; almost all of its pages are painted with a pair of miniatures. Each page is marked with two red circles to symbolize the places where in an Indian *pothi* manuscript the pages would have been pierced (See nos 19 and 20). This is the second in a series of volumes, as shown by the letter 'kha' written on each page and engraved on one of the short sides of the volume.

17   Five hymns addressed to five protective Buddhist goddesses
(SKT *Pancaraksa* and *Ratnaketudharani*)

Paper
287 ff
210 × 610 mm
One page illuminated with 7 miniatures
Text in Tibetan
Tibet
16th century

This manuscript, written in gold and silver on a highly polished dark blue paper, consists of the *Pancaraksa*, hymns to five protective Buddhist goddesses, and the *Ratnaketudharani*, another tantric text containing spells for the protection against evil. Instead of the more common wooden boards two thick card boards are used as covers. The first two pages, containing the title, are written in raised gold pigment and are protected by two layers of Indian silk. The very high-quality calligraphy of the manuscript is evenly spaced and nicely balanced. One page is illustrated with seven paintings in a sixteenth century style, representing the five goddesses flanked by two Tibetan lamas obviously associated with the transmission of the text. Their names, as they appear in the captions, are 'Jam pa'i dbyungs kun dga' grol mchog (1507–66), a famous Jo-nang-pa master, and mKhas grub rnam grol mtshan can.

18 The so-called Five Hundred Icons of Narthang
(TIB *Rin 'byung sNar thang brgya rtsa rdor 'phreng bcas nas gsungs pa'i bris sku: mthong ba don ldan bzhugs so*)

Paper
176 ff, 9 ff missing
115 × 170 mm
Each page with 3 illustrations
Text in Tibetan
Tibet
19th century

The so-called *Five Hundred Icons of Narthang* is the only block printed book in the exhibition. Its inclusion is justified both by its extreme interest and by its rarity, this being probably the sixth copy known of the text and the images. The book, compiled in the early nineteenth century, illustrates important tantric visions of the fourth Panchen Lama and has been one of the major sources for the iconographic study of the Buddhist pantheon in Tibet. Each numbered leaf has three illustrations in compartments, with captions containing the names of the represented deity. The accompanying mantra texts are printed on a different sheet of paper, and pasted to the back of the images, with a third blank sheet in between. Tachikawa published an enlarged facsimile of this work, based on the copy preserved in Hamburg, from which the nine pages missing from this copy and part of two further leaves have been photocopied. Most of the known copies of this book are incomplete and sometimes barely visible. The illustrations of this copy have all been solidly impressed from the original blocks, probably in the nineteenth century, and show a wealth of details missing in Tachikawa's facsimile.

19 Five hymns addressed to five protective Buddhist goddesses
(SKT *Pancaraksa*)

Wood and palm-leaf
151 ff, some missing
55 × 126 mm
Book covers illuminated
Text in Sanskrit
Nepal
13th–14th century.

The manuscript is a classical example of the Indo-Nepalese *pothi* format. The palm-tree leaves on which the text is written and the two wooden covers are pierced and held together by a string. The tantric text, a series of five hymns to five protective goddesses, is one of the most venerated in Indo-Tibetan Buddhism and the *puja* marks still visible on the exterior of the covers testify to the ritual use of this book. In the month of *Gumla* it is still common for Newar Buddhist community in Nepal to call the family priest for the daily reading of the family copy of the *Pancaraksa*. The present book is a high-quality example of such a family manuscript. Palaeographic evidence suggests a date in the second half of the thirteenth century or the beginning of the fourteenth. The inner face of the covers are decorated with representations of the five Tathagatas, the five cosmic Buddhas central to Mahayana cosmology, on one cover and the five goddesses on the other. The style of these images is extremely influential on Tibetan painting of the same period, as can be seen comparing one of the Tathagata's representation with the Buddha painted in the Dolpo manuscript no. 8. The two images, save for their size, are virtually interchangeable.

20 Five hymns addressed to five
protective Buddhist goddesses
(SKT *Pancaraksa*)

Palm-leaf
73 ff (4–22, 25–50, 62, 66–88)
60 × 540 mm
Two illustrated pages
Text in Sanskrit
India, Bihar
17th regnal year of King Madanapalla
(AD 1160)

This important Pala manuscript
of the *Pancaraksa*, dated to the
17th regnal year of king Madanapala
(AD 1160), displays the characteristics
of Pala book production and Pala
painting at their best. The colophon
leaf is now preserved, together with
another leaf, in the Los Angeles
County Museum. The exquisitely
balanced and powerful calligraphy
in *kutila* script is typical of manuscript
production of the twelfth century in
Bihar. The illustrations, representing
Mahasahasrapramardini (f. 5 r.)

and Mahamayuri (f. 88 r.), two of
the five protective goddesses the text
is dedicated to, are rare examples of
Pala painting, known now almost only
from book illuminations. The
goddesses are portrayed as if seen
through the doors of their shrines and,
despite their miniaturist scale, they
seem to project out of the page. This
remarkable three-dimensional effect
is achieved by the use of contrasting
bright colours to separate the planes
and by delicate shading in the bodies
of the figures. The manuscript once

belonged to Giuseppe Tucci and
is illustrated in his *Tibetan Painted
Scrolls*, Roma, 1949, vol. I, p. 274 and
pl. A. It was probably acquired in
the thirties, during one of his trips to
Tibet. This is the kind of manuscript
Indian masters would have brought
to Tibet or Tibetan pilgrims would
have collected in India at the
beginning of the second diffusion
of Buddhism in Tibet. The style of
its decoration would have had a
huge impact on the development
of Tibetan artistic traditions.

21 The Lotus of the True Law Sutra
(SKT *Saddharmapundarika sutra*,
CHN *Da cheng miao fa lian hua jing*)

Paper
7 volumes
334 × 118 mm
First and last volume illuminated
Text in Chinese
China
Ming dynasty, 16th–17th century

This luxurious manuscript in seven
volumes of the *Lotus Sutra*, one of the
most influential texts in East-Asian
Mahayana Buddhism, exemplifies the
Chinese tradition of *sutra* copying
in gold on indigo-blue paper. This
Chinese tradition could be the
source for the Tibetan and Nepalese
manuscripts in a similar technique,
which are known to have been
produced at least from the twelfth
century, in the early periods of the
second diffusion of Buddhism in
Tibet. The illustration at the beginning
of the first volume is a drawing in gold

pigment on blue paper in a crisp linear
style, with touches of malachite green
and azurite blue added to it in order to
highlight the borders of some robes
and the hair of some figures.
It represents the assemblies of
bodhisattvas and monks around the
Buddha who is preaching the *sutra*, a
subject not generally found in Tibetan
book illuminations. The last volume
ends with a second drawing in the same
style of the eight symbols of Buddhism,
followed by a monumental figure of
a *dharmaraja*. The style of these
paintings, which has a long history in

East-Asian Buddhist art, being attested
at least from the eight century in China
and Japan, has been considered a
possible origin for the Tibetan
tradition of black *thang-kas*,
the paintings in gold on black canvasses,
normally reserved for the protector
deities of Tibetan monasteries.
This hypothesis seems now to be
contradicted by the discovery of an
early black *thang-ka* in Pala style. The
presence of Tibetan consecrations in
the volumes prove that this copy of the
Lotus Sutra has became a ritual object
in a Tibetan context.

22 Book cover for a Perfection of Wisdom
manuscript

Wood – 695 × 194 × 18 mm
Tibet
12th–13th century

This cover is a superb example of
the best production of book covers
of the twelfth or thirteenth century,
at the beginning of the second
diffusion of Buddhism in Tibet.
The wooden inner surface of the
cover sharply contrasts with the plain
outer face for its rich decorations,
delicately carved in low relief and
painted with gold, silver and red
pigments. The cover most probably
belonged originally to

a *Prajnaparamita sutra* manuscript,
since the deity represented in the
middle of the central panel is the
four-armed goddess Prajnaparamita,
a personification of that text. She is
flanked on the left by Sakyamuni, the
historical Buddha, and on the right
by the Tathagata Vairocana, one of
the cosmic Buddhas. Between
these figures, in the loops of a floral
scroll stemming from the lotuses the
figures are sitting on, the 'Seven

emblems of royalty' are represented,
with an unusual eighth figure of
a dragon in the lower right corner,
most probably added in order to
preserve the symmetry of the
composition. The outer borders are
filled with luxuriant scrolls. In the
upper border they sprout from the
mouth of a *kirttimukha* and encase
jewels, while in the lower border they
are conceived as the tails of a pair of
mythological animals.

BIBLIOGRAPHY

Bhattacharya, Benoytosh, *The Indian Buddhist Iconography*, Calcutta: Firma K.L. Mukhopadhyay, 1958.

Chandra, Lokesh, *Buddhist Iconography of Tibet, Kyoto*: Rinsen Book Co., 1986.

Douglas, Nick, Tibetan Tantric Charms and Amulets, New York: Dover Publications.

Dowman, Keith, 'The Mandalas of the Lo Hampa Lhakhang' in Jane Casey Singer and Philip Denwood (eds.), *Tibetan Art. Towards a Definition of Style*, London: Laurence King Publishing, 1997, pp. 186-195.

Gomez, Luis O., Land of Bliss: *The Paradise of the Buddha of Measureless Light: Sanskrit and Chinese Versions of the Sukhavativyuha Sutra*, Honolulu: University of Hawaii Press, 1996.

Gyatso, Geshe Kelsang, *Guide to Dakini Land: A Commentary to the Highest Yoga Tantra Practices of Vajrayogini*, London: Tharpa Publications, 1991.

Heller, Amy, 'A Set of Thirteenth Century Tsakali', *Orientations*, 10, pp. 266–70, 1997.

Jackson, David, *A History of Tibetan Painting. The Great Tibetan Painters and Their Tradition*, Wien: Verlag der Österreichischen Akademie der Wissenschaften, 1996.

Kossak, Steven M. and Singer, Jane Casey (eds.), *Sacred Visions. Early Paintings from Central Tibet*, New York: The Metropolitan Museum of Art, 1998.

Losty, Jeremiah P., *The Art of the Book in India*, London: The British Library, 1982.

Mallmann, Marie-Therese de, *Etude iconographique sur Manjusri*, Paris: Ecole française d'Extreme-orient, 1964.

Neumann, Helmut, 'Paintings of the Lori Stupa in Mustang' in Jane Casey Singer and Philip Denwood (eds.), *Tibetan Art. Towards a Definition of Style*, London: Laurence King Publishing, 1997, pp. 178–85.

Pal, Pratapaditya and Meech-Pekarik, Julia, *Buddhist Book Illuminations*, New York-Hurstpierpoint Suss: Ravi Kumar Publishers-Richard Lyon, Chimera Books, 1988.

Rangdrol, Tsele Natsok, *Lamp of Mahamudra*, Boston & Sshaftesbury: Shambala Publications, , 1989.

Reynolds, Valrae, Heller, Amy and Gyatso, Janet, *Catalogue of the Newark Museum Tibetan Collection. Volume III: Sculpture and Painting*, Newark: The Newark Museum, 1986.

Roerich, George N., *The Blue Annals*, Delhi: Motilal Banarsidass, 1976.

Singer, Jane Casey and Denwood, Philip (eds.), *Tibetan Art. Towards a Definition of Style*, London: Laurence King Publishing, 1997.

Tachikawa, M., Mori, M. and Yamaguchi, S., *Five Hundred Buddhist Deities*, Osaka, 1995.

Thondrup Rinpoche, *Buddha Mind: An Anthology of Longchen Rabjam's Writings on Dzongpa Chenpo*, New York: Snow Lion Publications, 1989.

Tucci, Giuseppe, *Tibetan Painted Scrolls*, Roma: La Libreria dello Stato, 1949.

Vira, R. and Chandra, L., *A New Tibet-Mongol Pantheon*, New Delhi, 1964.

Wilson, M. and Brauen, M., *Deities of Tibetan Buddhism*, Boston, 2000.

Wayman, Alex, *Chanting the Names of Manjusri*, Boston & London: Shambala, 1985.

RECENT CATALOGUES

16 Text Manuscripts and Documents

17 India and the Himalayas

18 The Christian East

19 East Asian Books

20 Illuminated Manuscripts of the Middle Ages

21 Indian Paintings and Manuscripts

22 Islamic Manuscripts

23 Chinese Books

24 Ethiopian Art

CREDITS

DESIGN
Mark Vernon-Jones

PHOTOGRAPHY
Matt Pia

PRODUCTION
Robert Marcuson

Printed in UK

ISBN 0 9539422 2 8
Copyright 2001 Sam Fogg, London